SCHOLASTIC

Follow the Directions... and Learn!

Dozens of Ready-to-Go Pages That Help Kids Learn to Follow Directions—Independently!

BY DINA ANASTASIO

D0877847

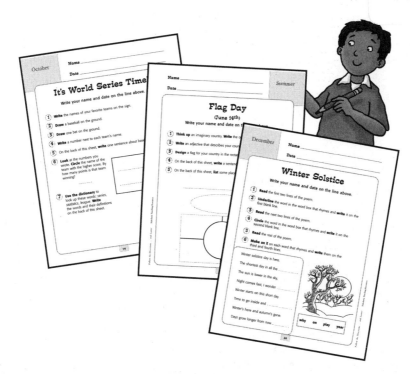

NEW YORK • TORONTO • LONDON • AUCKLAND • SYDNEY
MEXICO CITY • NEW DELHI • HONG KONG • BUENOS AIRES

Teaching *Resources*

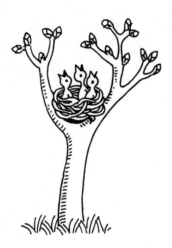

Cover and interior design by Holly Grundon
Cover illustration by Steve Cox
Interior illustration by George Ulrich

ISBN 0-439-40415-0
Copyright © 2004 by Dina Anastasio
All rights reserved.
Printed in the U.S.A.

2 3 4 5 6 7 8 9 10   40   11 10 09 08 07 06 05 04

Contents

Introduction 4

September
Wacky Backpack 6
Summer Reading 7
Labor Day 8
Grandparents Day 9
Here Comes Autumn 10

October
Columbus Day 11
Columbus Day Poem 12
United Nations Day 13
It's World Series Time! 14
Happy Halloween! 15
Halloween Cake 16
Election Day Is Coming! 17

November
If I Were President 18
Autumn Leaves 19
Ready for Winter 20
Happy Thanksgiving! 21
My Thanksgiving Menu 22

December
It's Snowing 23
Winter Solstice 24
Happy Holidays 25
Holiday Candle 26
New Year's Eve 27
Looking Back 28

January
Happy New Year 29
It's National Soup Month 30
Superbowl Scrapbook 31
Dr. Martin Luther King, Jr. Day 32
Everything's Frozen 33
Winter Words 34

February
Groundhog Day 35
Groundhog Day Weather 36
Valentine's Day 37
Valentine's Day Cupcakes 38
Presidents' Day 39
Mardi Gras 40

March
March Weather 41
Reading Month 42
My Autobiography 43
St. Patrick's Day 44
Luck of the Irish 45
Here Comes Spring! 46

April
April Fool! 47
Time Zones 48
April Clouds 49
Earth Day 50
Happy Spring! 51
Arbor Day 52

May
May Flowers 53
Space Day 54
Mars Explorer 55
Mother's Day Pancakes 56
Happy Mother's Day 57
Teacher's Day 58

Summer
Flag Day 59
Father's Day 60
Fourth of July 61
Friendship Day 62
Summer Olympics 63
Olympic Sports 64

Introduction

Welcome!

Following directions is a basic life skill. Everyone needs to be able to follow directions independently in order to complete everyday tasks. Directions help us to fill out applications, follow recipes, travel from here to there, complete forms, and assemble parts. And, following directions is crucial to success in the classroom. Children in particular need to follow directions in order to:

◎ complete activities correctly

◎ work independently

◎ complete class assignments and homework

◎ play games and sports

◎ solve puzzles

Sometimes, difficulty with following directions can hinder an otherwise capable student's performance. Here's the book you need to help children build these important skills all year long, especially those commonly given in the classroom:

◎ underlining

◎ circling

◎ filling in a blank

◎ making a check

◎ drawing

◎ numbering

◎ following a sequence

◎ using a dictionary

◎ making a list

Connections to the Standards

The activities in this book support the following language arts standards and benchmarks outlined by the Mid-continent Research for Education and Learning (McRel), a nationally recognized nonprofit organization that collects and synthesizes national and state K–12 standards.

⊕ Uses reading skills and strategies to understand a variety of informational texts.

⊕ Gives and responds to oral directions.

⊕ Gives and follows simple instructions in the target language.

Source: *Content Knowledge: A Compendium of Standards and Benchmarks for K–12 Education,* 4th Edition (Mid-continent Research for Education and Learning, 2003)

Using These Pages

These reproducible pages can be used anytime—for whole group instruction, small group, individual seatwork or even homework.

◎ Make a copy of the page for each student.

◎ If working with a student individually, sit quietly with him or her. Together, read each direction slowly and carefully. Have the student explain in his or her own words exactly what he or she is being asked to do.

◎ Remind students to write their name and the date at the top of their paper.

◎ Make sure that students understand and complete the first direction before moving on to the next.

◎ Have students check their work before moving on to the next direction.

◎ When the activity is complete, have students reread all the directions, check each detail, and make any necessary changes. For more strategies, see sidebar at right.

If Students Have Trouble

For a variety of reasons, following directions presents a special challenge for some students. In order to follow directions correctly, they must listen, read slowly and carefully, pay attention, and concentrate. Since remembering the sequence of several steps can be confusing, have students take one direction at a time and think about it until they understand exactly what they are being asked to do. You might have them check off each step as it is completed.

To demonstrate the real-life importance of following directions, you might ask students to dictate or write directions for a familiar task, such as making a peanut butter and jelly sandwich. Then, pantomime following their directions, making some obvious mistakes as you go (such as not taking the lid off the jar)!

Supporting Students Who Have Trouble Following Directions

Discuss your concerns with your school's learning specialist to determine if any testing should be recommended.

Provide both written and oral directions.

As much as possible, seat the student away from auditory or visual distraction.

Speak slowly and clearly, using words like *first*, *next*, *then* and *last*.

Avoid asking the student to write and listen simultaneously.

Start with single directions and gradually move to multi-step directions.

Use a highlighter to indicate the numbers of each step.

Stop periodically to ensure the student is on track.

Check yourself to assess the level of vocabulary you are using.

Have a peer act as a model for the struggling student.

Name _____

Date _____

Wacky Backpack

Write your name and date on the lines above.

(**1**) **Write** your name in the rectangle.

(**2**) **Write** the name of your favorite movie in the square.

(**3**) **Write** the name of your favorite team in the circle.

(**4**) **Write** the name of your favorite singer in the triangle.

(**5**) **Decorate** your backpack.

(**6**) On the back of this sheet, **list** three things that you would put in your backpack.

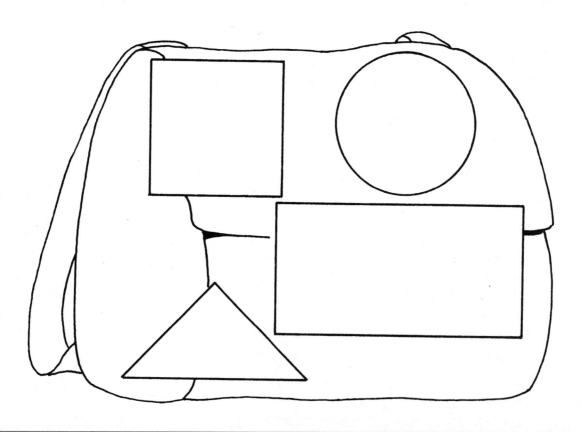

Summer Reading

Write your name and date on the lines above.

1. What is your favorite fiction book? **Write** the name on book 1.

2. What is your favorite nonfiction book? **Write** the name on book 2.

3. Who is your favorite author? **Write** the name on book 3.

4. Pretend you have written a book. **Write** its title on book 4.

5. How many books did you read this summer? **Write** the number in the triangle.

6. On the back of this sheet, **make a list** of the books you read this summer.

7. **Use the dictionary** to look up these words: *biography, autobiography, prose*. **Write** the words and their definitions on the back of this sheet.

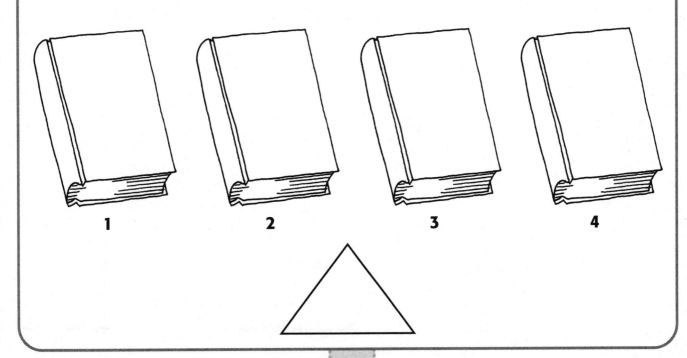

1   2   3   4

Name _____

Date _____

Labor Day

Write your name and date on the lines above.

(1) **Circle** the jobs you would like to do.

(2) **Make X's** on the jobs you would not like to do.

(3) **Write** your dream job on line 1.

(4) **Write** a job you would not like to do on line 2.

(5) On the back of this sheet, **make a list** of five more jobs that you might like to do.

(6) **Write** one sentence about your dream job.

(7) **Use the dictionary** to look up these words: *employment, occupation.* **Write** the words and their definitions on the back of this sheet.

1. _____

2. _____

florist

teacher

firefighter

storekeeper

musician

basketball player

doctor

Follow the Directions … and Learn! Scholastic Teaching Resources

Name _____

Date _____

Grandparents Day

(1st Sunday after Labor Day)

Write your name and date on the lines above.

(1) **Write** an adjective in box 1.

(2) **Write** a noun in box 2.

(3) **Write** verbs in boxes 3 and 4.

(4) **Decorate** the rest of your card.

(5) On the back of this sheet, **write** your own four-line poem for a grandparent or older relative.

(6) **Use the dictionary** to find the meaning of these words: *couplet, sonnet, epic.* **Write** the words and their definitions on the back of this sheet.

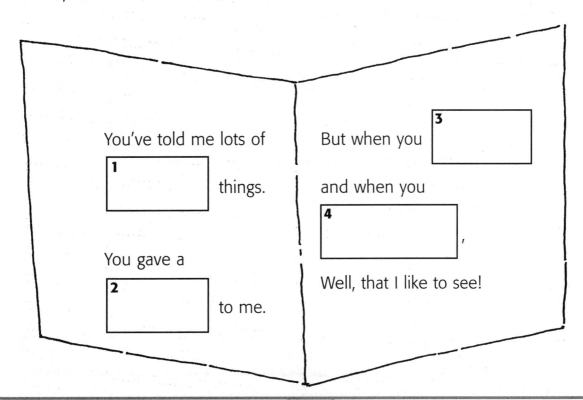

You've told me lots of

1

things.

You gave a

2

to me.

But when you

3

and when you

4

,

Well, that I like to see!

Name _____

Date _____

Here Comes Autumn

Write your name and date on the lines above.

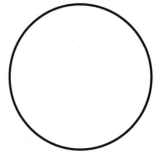

(1) On or about September 23rd, night and day are exactly the same length. This day is called the Autumnal Equinox. At about what time did the sun rise today? **Write** the time in the circle.

(2) How many hours of daylight will there be on this day? **Circle** the correct answer.

3   12   6

(3) How many hours of darkness will there be? **Circle** the correct answer.

8   12   9

(4) Check a calendar. **Circle** the date of this year's Autumnal Equinox below. **Make an X** on each of the other dates.

21   22   23   24   25   26   27   28   29

(5) On the back of this sheet, **make a list** of five changes that happen in autumn where you live.

Name _____

Date _____

Columbus Day
(2nd Monday in October)

Write your name and date on the lines above.

(1) Columbus sailed west. **Draw** a line from Spain to the Bahamas.

(2) Columbus sailed across an ocean. **Write** the name of the ocean on line 1.

(3) **Find** a picture of one of Columbus's ships in an encyclopedia or on the Web.

(4) **Draw** the ship on the ocean on this page.

(5) **Write** the name of the ship on line 2.

(6) **Color** the ocean blue.

(7) Where did Columbus sail to? **Write** the name on line 3.

UNITED STATES

Atlantic Ocean

Bahamas

EUROPE

Spain

_____   _____   _____
1   2   3

Name _____

Date _____

Columbus Day Poem

Write your name and date on the lines above.

1. **Read** the first two lines of the poem.

2. **Circle** the word in the box that rhymes and **write** it on the first blank line.

3. **Read** the next two lines of the poem. Underline the word in the box that rhymes and **write** it on the second blank line.

4. **Read** the last two lines of the poem.

5. **Make an X** on the word in the box that rhymes and **write** it on the third blank line.

6. On the back of this sheet, **write** your own Columbus poem.

Spain	**instead**	**find**

Christopher Columbus said "I've made up my mind!
I'll sail 'cross the ocean and guess what I'll _____ ?

A short route to Asia. There are spices!" he said.
But Columbus discovered the Bahamas _____ .

Then he sailed on to Cuba, through the warm autumn rain.
He discovered Hispaniola. Then he sailed back to _____ .

Follow the Directions ... and Learn!   Scholastic Teaching Resources

United Nations Day
(October 24th)

Write your name and date on the lines above.

(1) **Color** each stripe with a 1 on it red.

(2) **Color** each stripe with a 2 on it blue.

(3) On the back of this sheet, **write** the name of your own made-up country.

(4) **Draw** a red, white, and blue flag for your country.

(5) **Make** a list of five words that describe your country.

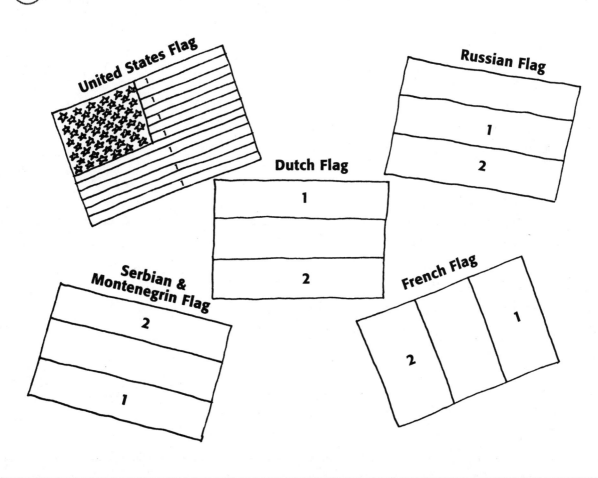

Name _____

Date _____

It's World Series Time!

Write your name and date on the lines above.

1   **Write** the names of your favorite teams on the sign.

2   **Draw** a baseball on the ground.

3   **Draw** one bat on the ground.

4   **Write** a number next to each team's name.

5   On the back of this sheet, **write** one sentence about baseball.

6   **Look** at the numbers you wrote. **Circle** the name of the team with the higher score. By how many points is that team winning?

_____

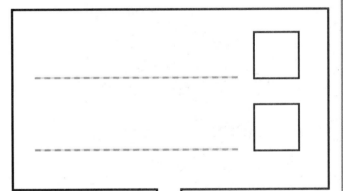

7   **Use the dictionary** to look up these words: *series*, *statistics*, *league*. **Write** the words and their definitions on the back of this sheet.

Follow the Directions ... and Learn!   Scholastic Teaching Resources

Happy Halloween!

Write your name and date on the lines above.

(1) **Draw** a weird hat on the trick-or-treater's head.

(2) **Draw** 6 different buttons on the trick-or-treater's jacket.

(3) **Make a check mark** (✔) next to the button you like best.

(4) **Color** the jacket and the hat the same color.

(5) **Color** the jacket and the trick-or-treat bag different colors.

(6) **Draw** 5 different pieces of candy on the bag.

(7) On the back of this sheet, **write** one sentence about the best costume you've ever worn.

Name _____

Date _____

Halloween Cake

Write your name and date on the lines above.

1. **Color** 3 pumpkins orange.

2. **Color** the stem on one of the orange pumpkins green.

3. **Color** 1 pumpkin green.

4. **Color** the cat black.

5. **Color** the moon yellow.

6. **Color** the haunted house 3 different colors.

7. **Make a check mark** (✓) on each thing that is yellow.

8. **Make an X** next to each thing that is green.

9. **Color** the background of the cake a light color.

Name _____

Date _____

Election Day Is Coming

Write your name and date on the lines above.

1 For whom would you vote for president? **Write** his or her name on line 1 of the Write-in Ballot.

2 **Write** the name of someone you'd like to be your mayor on line 2.

3 **Write** the name of someone you'd like to be your governor on line 3.

4 **Write** something you'd like to see change in your town or city on line 4.

5 On the back of this sheet, **describe** the change you would like to see.

Write-in Ballot

1. _____

2. _____

3. _____

4. _____

Name _____

Date _____

If I Were President

Write your name and date on the lines above.

1. **Find and circle** the spelling mistake.

2. **Correct** the spelling mistake.

3. **Write** a noun on line 1.

4. **Write** a verb on line 2.

5. **Write** a verb on line 3.

6. **Complete** the sentence on line 4.

7. On the back of this sheet, **write** 5 things that you would change if you were president.

My Presedential Platform

1. I would get rid of _____

_____ .

2. I would tax anyone who _____

_____ .

3. I would give medals to anyone who

_____

_____ .

4. I would promise to _____

_____

_____ .

Follow the Directions ... and Learn!   Scholastic Teaching Resources

Autumn Leaves

Write your name and date on the lines above.

(1) Evergreen leaves do not change color.
Draw two side-by-side evergreen leaves here:

(2) **Draw** a maple leaf next to your evergreen leaves.

(3) **Draw** three small oak leaves at the bottom of this page.

(4) **Draw** a birch leaf on the back of this page.

(5) How many leaves did you draw altogether on this page? _____

Name _____

Date _____

Ready for Winter

Write your name and date on the lines above.

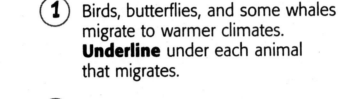

(**1**) Birds, butterflies, and some whales migrate to warmer climates. **Underline** under each animal that migrates.

(**2**) Bears, skunks, and some bats hibernate in the winter. **Circle** each animal that hibernates.

(**3**) Snakes, frogs, mice, and many insects keep warm in holes and under rocks. **Draw** three lines under each animal that burrows into a warm place.

(**4**) **Circle** the word "migrates" on this page. **Underline** the word "climates" on this page.

(**5**) **Use the dictionary** to look up these words: *migrate, hibernate, burrow*. **Write** the words and their definitions on the back of this sheet.

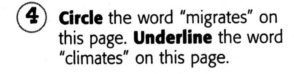

Follow the Directions ... and Learn!   Scholastic Teaching Resources

Happy Thanksgiving!

Write your name and date on the lines above.

1. **Write** relatives' names on the two square place cards.

2. **Write** friends' names on the two rectangular cards.

3. **Write** three made-up names on the two round cards.

4. **Decorate** the place cards and **color** the tablecloth.

5. On the back of this sheet, **write** a rhyming Thanksgiving couplet (two lines).

6. How many people are coming to this dinner? **Write** the number next to the title of this page.

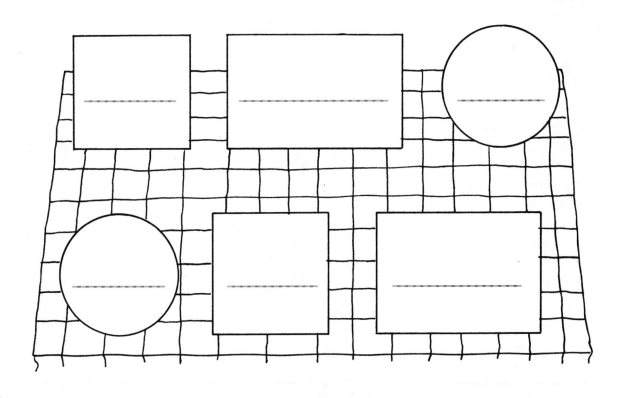

Name _____

Date _____

My Thanksgiving Menu

Write your name and date on the lines above.

(1) **Write** the name of a soup on line 1.

(2) Think of one ingredient in stuffing. **Write** it on line 2.

(3) **Write** the name of a vegetable on line 3.

(4) **Write** a type of potato on line 4.

(5) **Write** the name of your favorite pie on line 5.

(6) On the back of this sheet, **write** your own Thanksgiving menu.

(7) **Look at** your menu for thirty seconds and then **close your eyes**. Can you remember everything on your menu?

 1. _____

 2. _____

 3. _____

 4. _____

 5. _____

Follow the Directions ... and Learn! Scholastic Teaching Resources

It's Snowing

Write your name and date on the lines above.

1 **Draw** a hat on the snowman.

2 **Draw** a frozen pond under the snowman.

3 **Draw** a sun in the upper right corner of this page.

4 **Draw** 3 buttons on the snowman.

5 **Draw** 6 snowflakes above the snowman.

6 **Add** together the number of snowflakes and the number of buttons. **Draw** that many dots on the snowman's hat.

7 On the back of this sheet, **write** 6 words that rhyme with the word "snow."

8 **Write** a "snow" poem on the back of this sheet. Use some of the rhyming words you listed.

Follow the Directions ... and Learn!   Scholastic Teaching Resources

Name _____

Date _____

Winter Solstice

Write your name and date on the lines above.

(1) **Read** the first two lines of the poem.

(2) **Underline** the word in the word box that rhymes and **write** it on the first blank line.

(3) **Read** the next two lines of the poem.

(4) **Circle** the word in the word box that rhymes and **write** it on the second blank line.

(5) **Read** the rest of the poem.

(6) **Make an X** on each word that rhymes and **write** them on the third and fourth lines.

Winter solstice day is here.

The shortest day in all the _____ .

The sun is lower in the sky,

Night comes fast, I wonder _____ .

Winter starts on this short day.

Time to go inside and _____ .

Winter's here and autumn's gone.

Days grow longer from now _____ .

| why | on | play | year |

Follow the Directions ... and Learn!   Scholastic Teaching Resources

Happy Holidays

Write your name and date on the lines above.

1 To whom do you want to send your card? **Write** his or her name on the top line.

2 **Write** a four-word message on the middle line.

3 **Write** your first and last name on the bottom line.

4 **Circle** your first name.

5 **Make** a squiggly line under your last name.

6 **Invent** a holiday game. **Write** the name of your game on the back of this sheet.

7 Below the name of your game, **list** four directions that tell how to play it. **Number** your directions.

To: _____

_____

From: _____

Name _____

Date _____

Holiday Candle

Write your name and date on the lines above.

(1) **Draw** a candle holder for your candle.

(2) **Draw** three stars on your candle.

(3) **Draw** two circles on your candle.

(4) **Draw** another candle next to your candle. Make the second candle smaller.

(5) **Draw** four stars on the second candle.

(6) **Circle** the candle with the most stars.

(7) **Draw** a flame on one of your candles.

(8) **Print** your first name above the candle that does not have a flame.

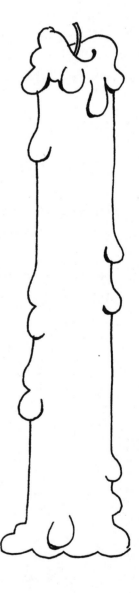

Follow the Directions ... and Learn! Scholastic Teaching Resources

New Year's Eve

Write your name and date on the lines above.

1. **Make a check mark** (✔) next to each New Year's Eve word in the box.

2. **Make an X** on each word that is not a New Year's Eve word.

3. **Write** the correct checked word on each blank line.

4. **Write** five more words that remind you of New Year's Eve on the back of this sheet.

5. **Write** a sentence using three of your words.

6. **Write** another sentence using the other two words.

7. **Circle** all five New Year's Eve words in your sentences.

Let's have a _____ ! Come on let's go!

The clock says _____ and it's not slow.

The month of _____ is really done.

Let's _____ and have some fun.

Soon the ball will slowly fall.

So Happy New _____ to you all!

December	party
midnight	autumn
summer	celebrate
Year	July
baseball	April

Name _____

Date _____

Looking Back

Write your name and date on the lines above.

(1) Where was the best place you went last year? **Write** it on line 1.

(2) What was the best book you read last year? **Write** the title on line 2.

(3) What was your favorite song last year? **Write** the name on line 3.

(4) What was your favorite TV show last year? **Write** the name on line 4.

(5) What was your favorite sport last year? **Write** it in the circle.

(6) What were the five best things that happened to you last year? **List** them on the back of this sheet.

(7) **Put** a star next to the very best thing that happened on your list.

1. -

2. -

3. -

4. -

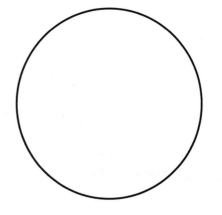

Name _____

January

Date _____

Happy New Year

Write your name and date on the lines above.

1 Want to be nicer to someone this year? **Write** his or her name on line 1.

2 Want to work harder at something this year? **Write** what it is on line 2.

3 Want to stop doing something this year? **Write** what it is on line 3.

4 Want to change something else this year? **Write** what it is on line 4.

5 **Use the dictionary** to look up these words: *resolution, prediction, transition.* **Write** the words and their definitions on the back of this sheet.

6 **Make a check mark (✓)** next to your most important New Year's resolution.

7 Think of three ways the world might change this year. **Write** your predictions on the back of this sheet.

8 **Number** your predictions.

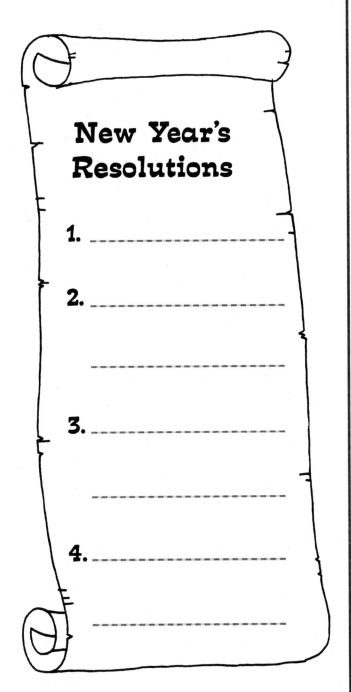

New Year's Resolutions

1. _____

2. _____

_____

3. _____

_____

4. _____

_____

Name _____

Date _____

It's National Soup Month

Write your name and date on the lines above.

1 **Use the dictionary** to look up these words: *ingredient, directions, measurement.* **Write** the words and their definitions on the back of this sheet.

2 **Circle** four ingredients you would like in your soup.

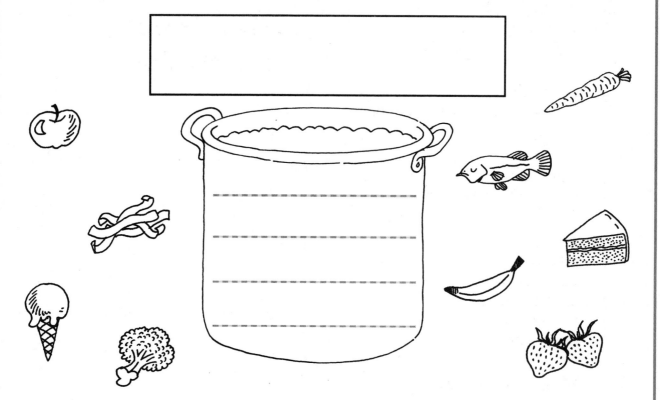

3 **Draw** a line from each of your ingredients to the soup pot.
Write the names of the ingredients on the lines.

4 **Make an X** on the picture of your favorite ingredient.

5 **Write** the name of your soup in the rectangle.

6 On the back of this sheet, **list** three steps that tell how to make your soup.

Follow the Directions ... and Learn! Scholastic Teaching Resources

Superbowl Scrapbook

Write your name and date on the lines above.

(1) **Draw** a Super Bowl ticket in the rectangle.

(2) **Write** a date on the ticket.

(3) **Draw** a football in the circle.

(4) **Write** a short newspaper football headline in the square.

(5) **Write** the names of two football teams in the triangle.

(6) **Predict** the score. **Write** the score near each team name.

(7) **Circle** the name of the winner.

(8) **Draw** a star next to the name of the winner.

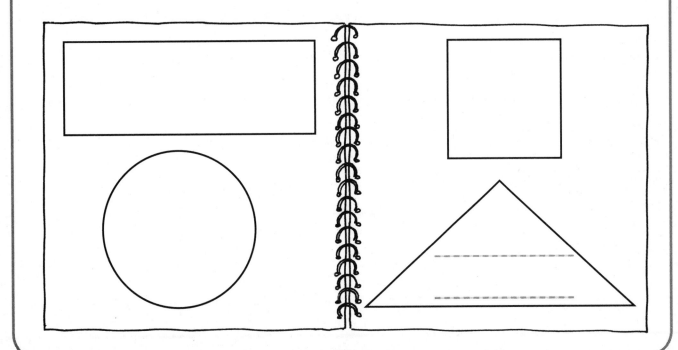

Name _____

Date _____

Dr. Martin Luther King, Jr. Day

(3rd Monday in January)

Write your name and date on the lines above.

1 **Write** a title relating to Dr. Martin Luther King, Jr. on the cover.

2 **Illustrate** your cover.

3 **Add** your name as the author.

4 On the back of this sheet, **print** your first name vertically. Using the letters in your name, **write** words or phrases that describe Martin Luther King. Make sure each word you choose starts with a letter in your first name.

5 On the back of this sheet, **write** one sentence telling what your book is about.

by _____

Follow the Directions ... and Learn!   Scholastic Teaching Resources

Everything's Frozen

Write your name and date on the lines above.

1. **Draw** three icicles hanging from the left side of the roof.

2. **Draw** four icicles hanging from the right side of the roof.

3. **Make an X** on the side of the roof with the most icicles.

4. **Make** three sets of bird prints in the snow.

5. **Color** all the snowflakes that look the same.

6. **Draw** a snowflake in the sky that looks the same as the ones you colored.

7. **Color** the door red.

Name _____

Date _____

Winter Words

Write your name and date on the lines above.

(1) Synonyms are words with similar meanings. **Circle** the word that means the same thing as "snowstorm."

(2) **Underline** the word that means "sleep through the winter."

(3) **Make a check mark** (✓) after the word that means "move on."

(4) **Make an X** on the word that means "frozen rain."

(5) **Draw** a line from the word *icy* to its synonym.

(6) On the back of this sheet, **list** three more winter words. **Write** a synonym next to each of your winter words.

(7) On the back of this sheet, **write** a sentence using three of your winter words.

blizzard   hibernate   icy

sleet   **MIGRATE**   solstice

ice hockey   **January**   **frozen**

Follow the Directions ... and Learn!   Scholastic Teaching Resources

Name _____

Date _____

Groundhog Day

(February 2nd)

Write your name and date on the lines above.

West   **East**

1. The sun rises in the east. **Draw** a morning sun around the word "East."

2. A shadow forms when light hits something solid. **Draw** the groundhog's shadow toward the west.

3. **Draw** the tree's shadow toward the west.

4. **Turn** this sheet over. **Print** the word *groundhog* in big letters at the top of the page.

5. Under each letter, **write** the name of another animal that starts with that letter. Write vertically.

6. **Create** a word-search puzzle using your animal names.

7. **Ask** a friend to do your puzzle.

Follow the Directions ... and Learn!   Scholastic Teaching Resources

Name _____

Date _____

Groundhog Day Weather

Write your name and date on the lines above.

1. **Make an X** in the Groundhog Day square.

2. **Use the dictionary** to look up these words: *forecast, meteorologist, blizzard*. **Write** the words and their definitions on the back of this sheet.

3. Forecast the weather for a week. **Write** a weather word in each of the seven squares that come after Groundhog Day.

4. Think back. **Write** a weather word for the day before Groundhog Day.

5. Pretend you're a meteorologist. On the back of this sheet, **write** three weather words that describe today's weather.

6. **Use** the three words in a sentence that describes today's weather.

February						
1	2 Groundhog Day	3	4	5	6	7
8	9	10	11	12	13	14
15	16	17	18	19	20	21
22	23	24	25	26	27	28

Follow the Directions … and Learn! Scholastic Teaching Resources

Name _____

Date _____

Valentine's Day

Write your name and date on the lines above.

1 **Read** the whole poem.

2 **Write** a name on line 1.

3 **Circle** the date in line 3.

4 **Draw** one line under a verb in line 4.

5 **Draw** two lines under a noun in line 4.

6 **Circle** the rhyming words in lines 5 and 6.

7 **Write** the name of a bird on line 8.

8 On the back of this sheet, **write** your own rhyming Valentine couplet.

Happy Valentine's Day

1. Hello, _____. It's Valentine's Day.

2. It all began in just this way.

3. On February 14th, quite long ago,

4. Someone noticed that in the snow

5. The birds came back and chose a mate,

6. Then someone decided to choose this date

7. To send a card to say "I love"

8. Just like the robin, _____, and dove.

Follow the Directions ... and Learn!   Scholastic Teaching Resources

Name _____

Date _____

Valentine's Day Cupcakes

Write your name and date on the lines above.

1. **Draw** 2 small hearts on cupcake 1.

2. **Draw** 1 large heart on cupcake 2.

3. **Circle** the cupcake with 3 hearts.

4. **Underline** the cupcake with 6 hearts.

5. **Turn** this sheet over. At the top of the page, **write** a name for your own special cupcake recipe.

6. In the middle of the page, **list** five ingredients that you will use to make your cupcakes.

7. At the bottom of the page, **list** three steps needed to make the cupcakes. **Number** your directions.

Follow the Directions … and Learn!   Scholastic Teaching Resources

Name _____

Date _____

Presidents' Day

Write your name and date on the lines above.

(1) **Underline** the name of the 16th president.

(2) **Make a check mark** (✔) next to the name of the first president.

(3) **Find** another president named George. **Make a check mark** (✔) next to his name.

(4) **Circle** all the presidents named James.

(5) **Make an X** next to each president named John.

(6) John Quincy Adams and George Walker Bush had fathers who were also presidents. **Underline** the names of the fathers.

(7) Turn this sheet over. **Write** your full name at the top of the page.

(8) On the back of this sheet, **write** one sentence describing why you would or would not like to be president.

Years	President
1789-1797	George Washington
1797-1801	John Adams
1801-1809	Thomas Jefferson
1809-1817	James Madison
1817-1825	James Monroe
1825-1829	John Quincy Adams
1829-1837	Andrew Jackson
1837-1841	Martin Van Buren
1841	William Henry Harrison
1841-1845	John Tyler
1845-1849	James Polk
1849-1850	Zachary Taylor
1850-1853	Millard Fillmore
1853-1857	Franklin Pierce
1857-1861	James Buchanan
1861-1865	Abraham Lincoln
1865-1869	Andrew Johnson
1869-1877	Ulysses Simpson Grant
1877-1881	Rutherford Birchard Hayes
1881	James Abram Garfield
1881-1885	Chester Alan Arthur
1885-1889	Grover Cleveland
1889-1893	Benjamin Harrison
1893-1897	Grover Cleveland
1897-1901	William McKinley
1901-1909	Theodore (Teddy) Roosevelt
1909-1913	William Howard Taft
1913-1921	Thomas Woodrow Wilson
1921-1923	Warren Gamaliel Harding
1923-1929	John Calvin Coolidge
1929-1933	Herbert Clark Hoover
1933-1945	Franklin Delano Roosevelt
1945-1953	Harry S Truman
1953-1961	Dwight David Eisenhower
1961-1963	John (Jack) Fitzgerald Kennedy
1963-1969	Lyndon Baines Johnson
1969-1974	Richard Milhous Nixon
1974-1977	Gerald Rudolph Ford
1977-1981	James (Jimmy) Earl Carter
1981-1989	Ronald Wilson Reagan
1989-1993	George Herbert Walker Bush
1993-2001	William (Bill) Jefferson Clinton
2001-	George Walker Bush

Name _____

Date _____

Mardi Gras

Write your name and date on the lines above.

1 **Color** the mouth on the mask.

2 **Draw** thin eyebrows on your mask.

3 To make the collar, **connect** the dots.

4 **Draw** three stars on the hat.

5 **Draw** a small bell on the end of each "arm" on the headpiece.

6 **Color** the headpiece and collar.

7 On the back of this sheet, **write** three words that describe your jester mask.

8 **Use** the three words in a sentence that describes your mask. **Write** your sentence on the back of this sheet.

Follow the Directions ... and Learn! Scholastic Teaching Resources

Name _____

Date _____

March Weather

Write your name and date on the lines above.

① **Look** at the symbols in squares 1 through 5.

② **Find** the matching words for the symbols in the word box.

③ **Write** the matching word in each of those squares.

④ **Make up** a symbol to match the word in square 6 and **draw** it in that square.

⑤ On the back of this sheet, **write** two words that describe a lion.

⑥ **Write** one word that describes a lamb.

⑦ **Write** a sentence explaining your understanding of the phrase "March comes in like a lion and goes out like a lamb."

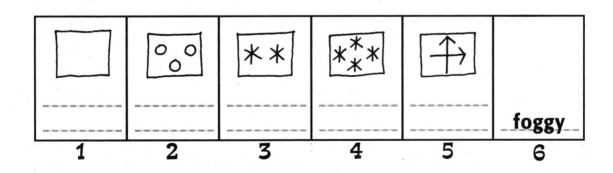

| rain | clear | heavy snow | light snow | blowing snow |

Follow the Directions ... and Learn!   Scholastic Teaching Resources

Name _____

Date _____

Reading Month

Write your name and date on the lines above.

(1) **Write** the title of your favorite biography on book 1.

(2) **Write** the name of the author of book 1 below the book.

(3) **Write** the title of your favorite mystery on book 2.

(4) **Write** the name of the book 2 author above the book.

(5) **Write** the title of your favorite fiction story on book 3.

(6) **Write** the title of your favorite sports book on book 4.

(7) **Draw** a picture on book 4 that shows what it is about.

(8) **Circle** the number below your very favorite book on the page.

1   2   3   4

Follow the Directions … and Learn!   Scholastic Teaching Resources

Name _____

Date _____

My Autobiography

Write your name and date on the lines above.

(1) **Write** one good thing about yourself on line 1.

(2) **Write** something that happened to you when you were a baby on line 2.

(3) **Write** something that happened to you when you were six on line 3.

(4) **Write** something that happened to you when you were eight on line 4.

(5) **Turn** this sheet over. **Print** your first and last names at the top of the page.

(6) **Circle** every other letter in your name. Start with the first letter.

(7) **Write** words that describe you. Make sure each word starts with one of the circled letters in your name.

(8) **Write** a sentence about yourself using three of your words.

1. _____

2. _____

3. _____

4. _____

Follow the Directions ... and Learn!   Scholastic Teaching Resources

43

Name _____

Date _____

St. Patrick's Day

Write your name and date on the lines above.

1 **Invent** a green drink. **Draw** it in the square. **Write** its name next to the square.

2 **Draw** a green vegetable in the rectangle.

3 **Draw** a green fruit in the circle. **Write** its name next to the circle.

4 **Create** your own green dessert. **Draw** it in the triangle. **Write** its name next to the triangle.

5 **Write** the names of two brand-new green creations on the back of this sheet.

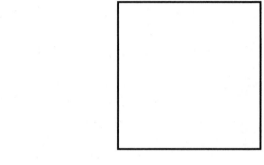

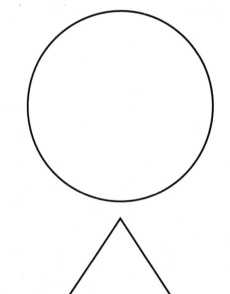

Follow the Directions ... and Learn!   Scholastic Teaching Resources

Luck of the Irish

Write your name and date on the lines above.

(1) A shamrock is a plant resembling clover. Most clovers have three leaves. A four-leaf clover means good luck. **Draw** a large four-leaf clover on the book cover. Leave room around your clover.

(2) **Draw** three small three-leaf clovers around your four-leaf clover.

(3) Your book is about luck. What do you want to call it? **Write** a title in the rectangle.

(4) **Circle** the clover at the bottom of the cover that is different from the others.

(5) **Color** the shamrocks any colors you like.

(6) On the back of this sheet, **draw** your own good luck charm.

Name _____

Date _____

Here Comes Spring!

Write your name and date on the lines above.

(1) **Make** a bird. For your bird's body, **draw** a large oval.

(2) **Add** a circle with a beak for the head.

(3) **Add** two tail feathers.

(4) **Add** two feet and a wing.

(5) **Draw** a line across the middle of the beak.

(6) **Add** your bird's eye.

(7) **Draw** a thought balloon above your bird's head. **Write** words in the balloon that show what your bird is thinking.

(8) On the back of this page, **write** a sentence telling why you would, or would not, enjoy flying like a bird.

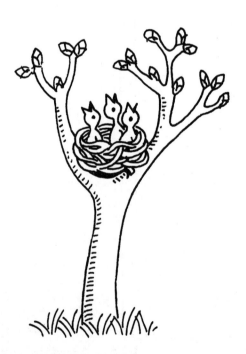

Follow the Directions ... and Learn!   Scholastic Teaching Resources

Name _____

Date _____

April Fool!

(April 1st)

Write your name and date on the lines above.

1. **Color** the square on the calendar that indicates April 1st.

2. **Write** the words APRIL FOOL backward on the banner. Start with the letter *L*.

3. **Circle** one thing that is wrong on this page.

4. **Make an X** on another thing that is wrong on this page.

5. **Cross out** your name at the top of this page. **Write** it again, backwards.

6. **Circle** the word *Trick* on this page. (Can't find it? April Fool!)

Name _____

Date _____

Time Zones

Write your name and date on the lines above.

(1) **Look** at the map. **Pretend** that it is 5 o'clock in the Eastern time zone.

(2) The Central time zone is 1 hour behind the Eastern time zone. **Write** the correct Central time here: _____

(3) Mountain time is 2 hours behind the Eastern time zone. **Write** the correct Mountain time here: _____

(4) Pacific time is 3 hours behind Eastern time. **Write** the correct Pacific time here: _____

(5) **Color** each time zone a different color.

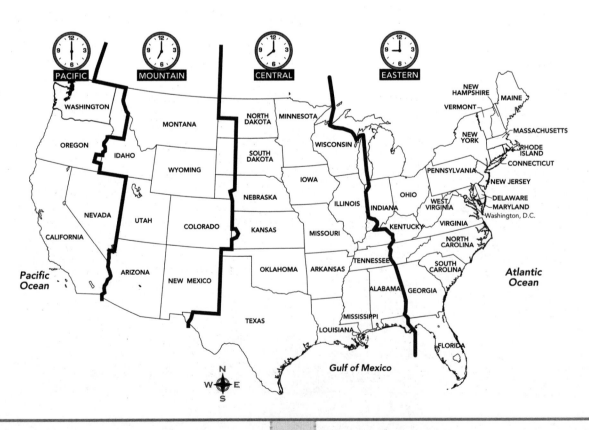

April Clouds

Write your name and date on the lines above.

(**1**) **Draw** a rock-shaped cloud in the sky above the little tree.

(**2**) **Draw** a donut-shaped cloud in the sky above the big tree.

(**3**) **Draw** a whale-shaped cloud in the sky above the medium-sized tree.

(**4**) On the back of this sheet, **draw** four clouds, each a different shape.

(**5**) **Ask** a friend to figure out what your clouds are shaped like.

(**6**) **Sign** your name in the bottom right corner on the back of this sheet.

Name _____

Date _____

Earth Day

Write your name and date on the lines above.

1 **Read** the poem.

2 **Using** the pictures below, **write** the name of the correct endangered species on each blank line.

3 **Circle** each endangered species after you **write** its name.

4 **Choose** one endangered species and **write** a poem about it on the back of this page. **Illustrate** your poem.

We're shrinking their homes. It doesn't seem fair.

What will become of the majestic _____ ?

Killed for their tusks, it's called ivory theft.

Before long there won't be an _____ left.

A small baby _____ needs a clean sea to grow.

Polluting its waters leaves it no place to go.

With few bamboo trees, it's safe to conclude,

You'll destroy a _____ and most of its food.

This species needs space to wander and roam.

We've endangered the _____ by shrinking its home.

Happy Spring!

Write your name and date on the lines above.

(**1**) **Write** "Happy Spring" on the large egg.

(**2**) **Draw** four small stars around the edge of the large egg.

(**3**) **Draw** a ribbon around the middle of the small egg.

(**4**) **Draw** six dots on the small egg.

(**5**) **Color** the two eggs different colors.

(**6**) **Draw** a nest for your eggs.

(**7**) On the back of this sheet, **write** a sentence about something important that happens in spring.

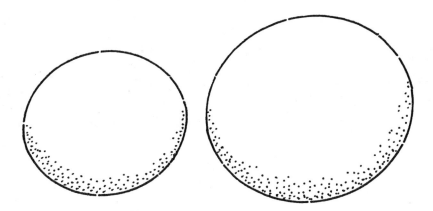

Name _____

Date _____

Arbor Day

Write your name and date on the lines above.

(1) A white pine tree has needles. **Circle** the white pine needles.

(2) The shagbark hickory tree has a compound leaf consisting of 5 small leaflets. **Draw** two lines under the shagbark hickory leaf.

(3) The American elm tree has simple oval leaves with jagged edges. **Make an X** on the American elm leaves.

(4) An English walnut tree has 7-9 leaflets. **Make a check mark** (✓) next to the English walnut leaflets.

(5) Using the words in the box, **write** the correct name under each leaf type.

_____   _____   _____   _____

_____   _____   _____   _____

| white pine | English walnut | American elm | shagbark hickory |

Name _____

Date _____

May Flowers

Write your name and date on the lines above.

(1) **Draw** three tall green stems at the bottom of the page.

(2) **Draw** a green oval leaf on either side of each stem.

(3) To make the flowers, **draw** petals on top of the stems.

(4) **Color** your flowers three different colors.

(5) **Draw** grass along the bottom of the page.

(6) On the back of this sheet, **draw** another flower any way you like.

(7) **Write** directions telling how to draw your flower.

(8) **Number** your directions.

Name _____

Date _____

Space Day

(May 3rd)

Write your name and date on the lines above.

① **Circle** the planet that is closest to the sun.

② **Underline** the largest planet.

③ **Make an X** on the smallest planet.

④ **Draw** a square around the planet farthest from the sun.

⑤ **Make a check mark** (✔) above the planet with a ring around it.

⑥ **Color** Mars red.

⑦ **Color** Neptune blue.

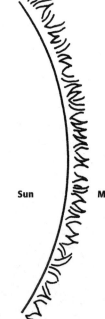   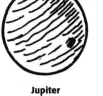

Sun   Mercury Venus Earth Mars   Jupiter   Saturn   Uranus   Neptune   Pluto

Mars Explorer

Write your name and date on the lines above.

1. On the left side of the page, **draw** a sample-collecting rover vehicle with six wheels.

2. **Draw** an antenna on your rover.

3. **Draw** a camera on your rover.

4. **Draw** a scoop at the front of your rover.

5. On the right side of the picture, **draw** three more rocks.

6. **Write** a sentence about whether or not you would like to be on a space expedition like this one.

7. **Color** the surface of Mars brown.

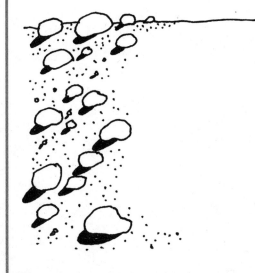

Name _____

Date _____

Mother's Day Pancakes

Write your name and date on the lines above.

(1) **Write** your mother's name on the line in the pancake.

(2) **Color** the pancake.

(3) **Make a check mark** (✓) next to the smallest measuring tool at the bottom of this page.

(4) **Read** the recipe. **Circle** the spelling mistakes.

(5) On the back of this sheet, **correct** the spelling mistakes.

◎ 1 cup flour

◎ 1 tablespoon butter

◎ 2 eggs

◎ 1/2 teaspoon salt

◎ 1/2 cup blueberries

◎ 1/4 cup milk

Mix all ingredients towgether. Pour onto hot griddle and use a spatula to flip ovar. Surve hot. Enjoy!

Happy Mother's Day

Write your name and date on the lines above.

1. **Color** the first letter of each word red.

2. **Color** the second letter of each word blue.

3. **Color** the last letter of each word green.

4. **Color** the rest of the letters any colors you like.

5. On the back of this sheet, **write** one adjective that begins with each of the red letters.

6. On the back of this sheet, **write** one noun that begins with each of the green letters.

7. On the back of this sheet, **write** the words on the banner in alphabetical order.

8. **Circle** the word on the banner that has the fewest letters.

Follow the Directions ... and Learn!   Scholastic Teaching Resources

Name _____

Date _____

Teacher's Day

Write your name and date on the lines above.

(1) Write a letter on line 1.

(2) Write a number on line 2.

(3) Write the name of a color on line 3.

(4) Write a time on line 4.

(5) Write the name of a month on line 5.

(6) On the back of this sheet, **write** three more things you would do if you were a teacher.

(7) Sign your name at the bottom right of your list.

---

1. If I were a teacher, I would always write the letter _____ on tests.

2. If I were a teacher, a school day would be _____ hours long.

3. If I were a teacher, all students would wear _____ on Fridays.

4. If I were a teacher, school would end at _____ o'clock every day.

5. If I were a teacher, there would be no school during the

month of _____.

Follow the Directions … and Learn!   Scholastic Teaching Resources

Flag Day

(June 14th)

Write your name and date on the lines above.

1. **Think up** an imaginary country. **Write** the country's name on the line below.

2. **Write** an adjective that describes your country in the oval.

3. **Design** a flag for your country in the rectangle.

4. **Draw** a symbol in the circle.

5. On the back of this sheet, **write** a sentence about your country.

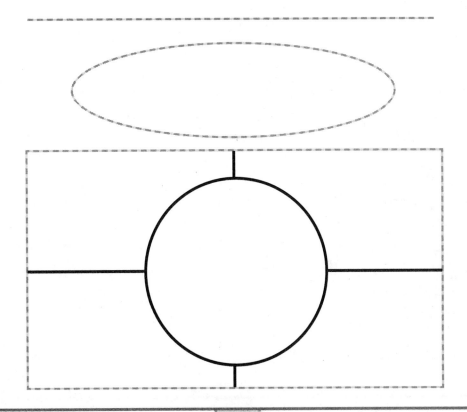

Name _____

Date _____

Father's Day

(3rd Sunday in June)

Write your name and date on the lines above.

1. **Circle** each item you would put in a Father's Day sandwich.

2. **Make an X** on each item you would not put in the sandwich.

3. **Write** three more possible ingredients on the lines.

4. **Circle** your favorite ingredient on the page.

5. On the back of this sheet, **write** directions for how to make your sandwich.

6. **Number** your directions.

--------   --------   --------

Fourth of July

Write your name and date on the lines above.

① **Read** the first two lines of the poem.

② **Write** the rhyming word from the box on the first blank line.

③ **Read** the next two lines.

④ **Write** the word that rhymes on the second blank line.

⑤ **Read** the rest of the poem.

⑥ **Write** the words that rhyme on the third and fourth blank lines.

⑦ On the back of this sheet, **write** one sentence that describes how the flag has changed since 1777.

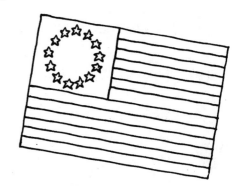

white	star	proclaimed	blue

The American Flag

In 1777 the nation was new,

So they made up a flag that was red, white and _____.

There were 13 states then. The flag waved day and night,

With 13 white stars, and stripes red and _____

Time passed and the flag stayed the same.

And then in the year 1818 they _____,

Since the union was adding new states near and far,

For each state there'd be one new white _____.

Name _____

Date _____

Friendship Day

(1st Sunday in August)

Write your name and date on the lines above.

A B C D E F G H I J K L M N

O P Q R S T U V W X Y Z

1. **Circle** the letters in a friend's first name.

2. **Make an X** on each letter in your first name.

3. **Write** the first letter of your friend's first name in each circle below.

4. **Write** the first letter of your first name in each square.

5. **Use the dictionary** to look up these words: *affable, jocular, loyal.*
   Write the words and their definitions on the back of this sheet.

6. **Circle** the word in #5 that best describes your friend.

7. On the back of this sheet, **list** four more adjectives that describe a good friend.

Follow the Directions … and Learn! Scholastic Teaching Resources

Name _____

Date _____

Summer Olympics

Write your name and date on the lines above.

(1) The Olympic flag has five interlocking rings. The rings represent five regions of the world: Australia, Africa, the Americas, Asia, and Europe. **Color** ring 1 blue.

(2) **Color** ring 2 black.

(3) **Color** ring 3 red.

(4) **Color** ring 4 yellow.

(5) **Color** ring 5 green.

(6) **Write** a different region in each ring.

(7) On the back of this sheet, **write** a sentence telling why you would or would not like to participate in an Olympic sport.

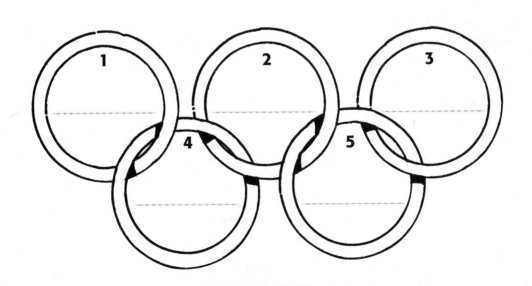

Name _____

Date _____

Olympic Sports

Write your name and date on the lines above.

(1) **Circle** your favorite summer Olympic sport.

(2) **Underline** your second favorite sport.

(3) **Write** the number 3 next to your third favorite sport.

(4) **Make an X** on each of the three sports you would not like to play.

(5) **Make a star** next to the sport you are best at.

(6) On the back of this sheet, **design** and **draw** your own Olympic Medal.

(7) **Write** one sentence that describes your medal.

Aquatics	Hockey
Archery	Judo
Athletics	Modern Pentathlon
Badminton	Rowing
Baseball	Sailing
Basketball	Shooting
Boxing	Softball
Canoeing/kayaking	Table Tennis
Cycling	Taekwondo
Equestrian	Tennis
Fencing	Triathlon
Football	Volleyball
Gymnastics	Weightlifting
Handball	Wrestling